I GREW UP TO BE
PRESIDENT

Laurie Calkhoven

Illustrated by Rebecca Zomchek

SCHOLASTIC INC.
NEW YORK • TORONTO • LONDON • AUCKLAND
SYDNEY • MEXICO CITY • NEW DELHI • HONG KONG

Text copyright © 2011 by Laurie Calkhoven
Illustrations copyright © 2011 by Scholastic Inc.
All presidential portraits courtesy of
the White House Historical Association.

All rights reserved. Published by Scholastic Inc., *Publishers since 1920*. SCHOLASTIC and associated logos are trademarks and/or registered trademarks of Scholastic Inc.

No part of this publication may be reproduced, stored in a retrieval system, or transmitted in any form or by any means, electronic, mechanical, photocopying, recording, or otherwise, without written permission of the publisher. For information regarding permission, write to Scholastic Inc., Attention: Permissions Department, 557 Broadway, New York, NY 10012.

ISBN 978-0-545-33152-4

10 9 8 7 6 5 4 3 2 1   11 12 13 14 15

Printed in the U.S.A.   40
First edition, December 2011
Cover design by Steve Scott
Interior design by Kay Petronio

Contents

Introduction

The thirteen American colonies won their independence from Great Britain in 1783, as a result of the American Revolution. Once they were free, they came together as the United States of America. The leaders of this new country, the Founding Fathers, knew that if the United States was going to survive, they had to create a strong central government to make laws and decide how the country would be run.

Representatives from each state had a meeting in Philadelphia in May 1787, called the Constitutional Convention, to talk about how this new government would work. The talks they had were so secret that many of the windows in Independence Hall, where the convention was held, were nailed shut. Four months later, they presented the American people with the Constitution of the United States, a document that explained how the new government would function.

This new government had three branches: a legislative branch to make laws, a judicial branch to oversee the courts, and an executive branch led by the president. The representatives at the Constitutional Convention unanimously elected George Washington the first president of the United States.

Since 1789, when Washington was elected, there have been forty-four presidents. Every four years, the people of the United States cast their votes to decide who will be president. Some of these men, such as Abraham Lincoln and Franklin D. Roosevelt, have led the country through difficult times of war and crisis. Others have led the American people during times of peace, freedom, and prosperity. All of them have worked to make the United States of America a stronger and better place.

George Washington

1st President
1789–1797

fact file

Born: February 22, 1732, near Pope's Creek, VA

Wife: Martha Dandridge Custis

Children: Stepfather to John, Martha

Political Party: Federalist

Vice President: John Adams

Died: December 14, 1799, at Mount Vernon, near Old Town, VA

George Washington grew up on a farm in Virginia. Exploring the woods was one of his favorite things to do, especially on horseback. Washington also had lessons in reading, writing, and arithmetic. He didn't have enough money to go to college, so he became a surveyor and drew maps of the Virginia wilderness.

In 1759, Washington married Martha Dandridge Custis and they settled down at Mount Vernon for a peaceful life of farming and local politics. But the colonists grew unhappy with Great Britain. They paid high taxes but had no say in the British government. When leaders from the thirteen colonies met in Philadelphia at the Continental Congress in 1774 to discuss what to do about the problem, Washington joined them.

War broke out during the second Continental Congress. Washington was asked to lead the new army against Great Britain. He was leading that army when the Continental Congress declared independence from Britain.

When the war ended in 1783, Washington traveled back to Virginia, but it wasn't long before his country needed him again. The thirteen colonies had become thirteen states, and they needed a strong central government to hold them together. Washington was the one man whom everyone trusted enough to do the job. He would have rather stayed at Mount Vernon, but Washington agreed to become the first president of the United States.

Washington was president for eight years. By the end of his second term, the thirteen colonies had become the United States of America, and George Washington had become known as the father of his country.

★ Washington's Teeth

By the time he was president, Washington had only one real tooth left. His many sets of false teeth were made from hippopotamus, walrus, and elephant ivory, and cow, elk, donkey, horse, and human teeth.

★ "Father, I Cannot Tell a Lie."

Washington's first biographer, Mason Locke Weems, wrote a story about young Washington cutting down a cherry tree with his hatchet. He said that Washington confessed with the words "Father, I cannot tell a lie." It became one of the most famous stories about young Washington, but it wasn't true. Weems didn't know very much about Washington's childhood, so he made things up!

John Adams

★★★★★

2nd President
1797–1801

fact file

Born: October 30, 1735, in Braintree (now Quincy), MA

Wife: Abigail Smith

Children: Abigail, John Quincy, Susanna, Charles, Thomas

Vice President: Thomas Jefferson

Political Party: Federalist

Died: July 4, 1826, in Quincy, MA

John Adams was born in the Massachusetts Bay colony in 1735. Growing up, he did well in school, but he was happier outdoors. His favorite hobby was hunting. Flying kites, sailing toy boats, and shooting marbles were other games he liked. He also loved to read.

Adams went to Harvard University and studied with a lawyer to become a lawyer himself. When trouble broke out with Great Britain, Adams went to the Continental Congress in 1774 in Philadelphia along with his cousin Samuel to discuss the problems with representatives from other colonies. He quietly talked about breaking away from Britain and asked Thomas Jefferson to write the Declaration of Independence.

Adams spent most of the revolution in Europe asking countries like France and the Netherlands for help. After the war he stayed in Europe to sign the peace treaty between Britain and the United States.

Adams, who was George Washington's vice president, thought the vice president's job was boring. When Washington stepped down, Adams ran for president against Jefferson. He beat Jefferson by only three votes! Adams spent most of his time in office trying to keep the country out of a war with France. His own political party was divided over the issue, while Jefferson's Democratic-Republicans were united in favor of peace. When Adams ran for a second term after four years, he lost to Jefferson.

★ Remember the Ladies

Adams's wife, Abigail, was one of the people he turned to when he needed advice. At a time when the laws of the land gave all the power to men, she believed that women should have rights, too. When her husband was at the Continental Congress, she wrote him a famous letter and told him to "remember the ladies."

★ Independence Day

Adams and Jefferson were the only two signers of the Declaration of Independence who went on to become president. They both died on the same day—July 4, 1826—exactly fifty years after they signed the Declaration.

★ The White House

Adams was the first president to live in the White House. When he and Abigail Adams moved in, the house was known as the President's House, and it was cold and unfinished. Many people called it the White House because of its color, but it wasn't officially known as the White House until 1901.

Thomas Jefferson

3rd President
1801–1809

fact file

Born: April 13, 1743, in Goochland County, VA

Wife: Martha Wayles Skelton

Children: Martha, Jane Randolph, Mary, Lucy Elizabeth, two children who died in infancy

Political Party: Democratic-Republican

Vice President: 1st term Aaron Burr; 2nd term George Clinton

Died: July 4, 1826, at Monticello, near Charlottesville, VA

Thomas Jefferson's father, Peter, was a surveyor and plantation owner in Virginia, like George Washington. Peter Jefferson took his son hunting and fishing, and told him stories about adventures in the wilderness.

Young Jefferson liked playing the violin. He also loved learning. When he was nine, he left home to go to school. Later, he became a lawyer and entered Virginia politics. He also built a home on "Tom's Mountain," his favorite spot, and called it Monticello.

Jefferson was a shy speaker, but an excellent writer. When the Congress decided to tell Great Britain they wanted independence, John Adams asked Jefferson to write the document. Nearly every member of the Congress signed what became known as the Declaration of Independence.

After the war, Jefferson became the United States' ambassador to France and was George Washington's first secretary of state. In 1796, he was elected vice president, and in 1800, he was elected president.

One of Jefferson's biggest accomplishments as president was the Louisiana Purchase. He bought a huge area of land in North America from the French—and doubled the size of the United States! Then Jefferson sent two explorers, Meriwether Lewis and William Clark, to explore the west and to find a route to the Pacific Ocean.

After two terms in office, Jefferson retired to Monticello, where he worked on his house and started the University of Virginia.

★ A Wild Gift

Jefferson had heard about grizzly bears from Lewis and Clark, but he never expected to see one at the White House. Then, in October 1807, explorer Zebulon Pike sent the president an unusual gift: two grizzly bear cubs! The bears lived on the White House grounds until Jefferson arranged to send them to a museum.

★ Library of Congress

Jefferson loved books. During the War of 1812, the British set fire to the Capitol and destroyed the government's library, the Library of Congress. Jefferson sold his vast library of more than six thousand books to the country so that the library could be restored.

James Madison

4th President
1809-1817

fact file

Born: March 16, 1751, in Port Conway, VA

Wife: Dolley Payne Todd

Children: None

Political Party: Democratic-Republican

Vice President: 1st term George Clinton; 2nd term Elbridge Gerry

Died: June 28, 1836, in Montpelier, VA

James Madison was born on a plantation in Virginia, the oldest in a family of eight children. Young Madison was often sick, and studied with private tutors.

In 1769, Madison left Virginia to study at the College of New Jersey (now Princeton University). He worked hard and graduated in only two years.

Madison went home and got involved in politics. When the colonies won the Revolution, Madison knew that the United States would need a central government. He was one of the first to ask, "What's next?"

While the states were deciding what that government would be like, Madison went to Philadelphia to help write the Constitution. In March 1789, the new Constitution became the law of the land. Afterward he was elected to Congress and fought to protect people's freedoms with the Bill of Rights.

President Jefferson asked his good friend Madison to be his secretary of state and later helped Madison get elected president in 1809. At the time, Britain was at war with France. Both countries tried to pull the United States into war. Madison was forced to declare war on Britain in 1812. The British set fire to the White House and the Capitol in 1814, but the president was unharmed. The war ended with an American victory.

After two terms, Madison followed in the footsteps of presidents Washington and Jefferson and retired to Virginia.

★ Strange But True

During his time with the Continental Congress, and later while he was secretary of state, Madison worried that people would read his letters. He used a tricky secret code when he wrote to Thomas Jefferson and other friends.

★ Ice Cream

The Madisons served a new dish at Madison's first inauguration. Most people had never tasted it before, but they must have thought it was delicious. It was ice cream!

★ Did You Know?

Madison was the smallest president. He was only 5 feet 4 inches tall and weighed less than 100 pounds. Many people worried that Madison's body was too weak to hold such an important job, but he had a very strong mind.

James Monroe

5th President
1817–1825

fact file

Born: April 28, 1758, in Westmoreland County, VA

Wife: Elizabeth Kortright

Children: Eliza Kortright, James Spence, Maria Hester

Political Party: Democratic-Republican

Vice President: Daniel D. Tompkins

Died: July 4, 1831, in New York, NY

James Monroe was born on his family's plantation in Virginia. He grew up roaming the woods and marshes and playing with his siblings.

He was attending college when the American Revolution began. Monroe and some friends raided the local armory, where the British kept their weapons. They presented two hundred stolen muskets and three hundred stolen swords to the Virginia militia to fight the British with. Then Monroe joined the Continental army. He fought with General Washington at the Battle of Trenton, and survived the difficult winter at Valley Forge.

When he returned to Virginia, Monroe studied law with Thomas Jefferson. He became a senator, a governor, and a diplomat. Later he helped President Jefferson buy the Louisiana Territory and worked as President Madison's secretary of state and secretary of war.

In 1817, he became president himself. Five new states joined the nation while Monroe was president. When Missouri asked to enter the Union as a slave state, there was a big debate. People who were against slavery didn't want any more slave states. They wanted more free states. Congress reached an agreement called the Missouri Compromise. Missouri was admitted as a slave state, with Maine joining the Union at the same time as a free state. Western territories, north of Missouri's southern border, would be free.

At the end of two terms, Monroe retired to Virginia. Like presidents Adams and Jefferson before him, he died on an anniversary of the nation's birth—July 4, 1831.

★ Hands Off!

Monroe bought the land that is now Florida from Spain. Then in 1823 he made a speech promising to stay out of Europe's business if Europe stayed out of the United States'. He told European leaders not to start any new colonies in North or South America. This policy is known as the Monroe Doctrine.

★ Did You Know?

Lieutenant James Monroe crossed the Delaware River with George Washington on December 25, 1776. He was wounded at the Battle of Trenton, and carried a bullet in his shoulder for the rest of his life.

John Quincy Adams

6th President
1825–1829

fact file

Born: July 11, 1767, in Braintree (now Quincy), MA

Wife: Louisa Catherine Johnson

Children: George Washington, John, Charles Francis, Louisa Catherine

Political Party: Democratic-Republican

Vice President: John C. Calhoun

Died: February 23, 1848, in Washington, DC

John Quincy Adams grew up hearing about the trouble between the colonies and Britain from his parents, John and Abigail Adams. Their home in Massachusetts was close enough to the Battle of Bunker Hill that young Adams watched the battle and heard the cannons roar.

When his father was sent to Europe during the Revolution, ten-year-old Adams went, too. He sat in on talks between his father and other leaders, including Benjamin Franklin and Thomas Jefferson. Later, Adams went to Harvard, studied law, and became a senator and a diplomat. His greatest achievement came when he was President Monroe's secretary of state and he helped create the Monroe Doctrine.

In 1824, Adams ran for president against Andrew Jackson and two other men. None of the candidates had enough votes to win. When that happens, the Constitution calls for the House of Representatives to decide the matter. Adams was named the winner.

He lost the election for a second term four years later, so he ran for Congress in order to fight against slavery. He is the only president to serve in the House of Representatives after leaving the White House. He was at the Capitol when he collapsed at his desk. He was taken care of in a nearby office and died two days later.

★ Dangerous Sea Voyages

Adams first crossed the Atlantic Ocean with his father when he was ten. Along the way the ship was struck by lightning, battered by a hurricane, and attacked by British ships. On his second voyage to Europe, the boat sprang a leak. Adams helped man the pumps to keep the ship afloat until it reached the coast of Spain.

★ Strange But True

As president, Adams took early morning swims in the Potomac River—nude! Once, someone stole his clothes and he had to ask a boy to go to the White House and get him something to wear.

★ Presidential Pets

The Marquis de Lafayette, a famous Revolutionary War hero, brought President Adams a pet alligator. The alligator lived in the White House for several months.

Andrew Jackson

7th President

1829–1837

fact file

Born: March 15, 1767, in the Waxhaw border region of North and South Carolina

Wife: Rachel Donelson Robards

Children: None

Vice President: 1st term John C. Calhoun; 2nd term Martin Van Buren

Political Party: Democrat

Died: June 8, 1845, in Nashville, TN

Andrew Jackson was born in a log cabin on the American frontier shortly after his father died. His mother was poor and uneducated, but Jackson had some schooling. When he was nine, he read the Declaration of Independence aloud to neighbors who had never learned to read themselves.

At thirteen, Jackson left school to join the American Revolution as a messenger. He was captured by the British and became a prisoner of war. Afterward, he tried different jobs before he decided to study law. He also started a cotton plantation in Tennessee, called the Hermitage.

Jackson led troops to victory in the Battle of New Orleans, the final battle in the War of 1812, and became a war hero. That made him a popular candidate for president. He was the first president who didn't come from a wealthy family, and that made the American people believe that anyone could succeed. The public loved him, but politicians were shocked by his bold actions. Instead of letting Congress lead the way in passing new laws, Jackson took charge and vetoed bills he didn't like. Only one major law, the Indian Removal Act, was passed in his eight years in office.

After two terms in office, Jackson retired to the Hermitage.

★ Old Hickory

Jackson's soldiers nicknamed him Old Hickory during the War of 1812 because he was as tough as the wood of a hickory tree. On the march, he was willing to suffer the same hardships as the average soldier and even gave up his horse to a wounded man.

★ Party Time!

Jackson was so popular that as many as twenty thousand fans stormed the White House for his inauguration party. The party got so wild that Jackson had to escape out a back door and go to a hotel. White House workers couldn't get the people to leave. Finally they put tubs of punch out on the lawn. When the partygoers went outside, the White House staff locked the doors and windows so they couldn't come back!

Martin Van Buren

8th President
1837–1841

fact file

Born: December 5, 1782, in Kinderhook, NY

Wife: Hannah Hoes

Children: Abraham, John, Martin, Winfield Scott, Smith Thompson

Vice President: Richard M. Johnson

Political Party: Democrat

Died: July 24, 1862, in Kinderhook, NY

Martin Van Buren grew up in Kinderhook, New York, where he was educated in a one-room schoolhouse. His family couldn't afford college, so Van Buren worked as a law clerk. He swept floors, ran errands, and studied law at night.

Van Buren's father ran a tavern where people came to talk about politics. Young Van Buren grew up listening to the discussions, and as soon as he became a lawyer, he got involved in politics himself. He was a state senator, a U.S. senator, and the governor of New York. Van Buren became Andrew Jackson's secretary of state during his first term and vice president in his second.

Van Buren won the 1836 election by promising to continue Jackson's policies. He didn't know that banks and businesses all over the country would begin to fail in the Panic of 1837. Thousands of Americans lost their jobs because of the Panic. Even though Van Buren didn't cause the problem, he got the blame. He lost the election for a second term, but he didn't give up. He ran for president twice more, once for a new antislavery party called the Free Soil Party. He lost both times. Finally, he retired to Kinderhook and died during the Civil War.

★ Did You Know?

Van Buren was the first president to be born an American citizen. Earlier presidents were all born before the American Revolution and were British subjects before the war.

★ Music Man

Van Buren loved to sing—loudly. His voice could often be heard above everybody else's in church.

★ Nicknames

Van Buren had a few nicknames over the years. One was the Little Magician because he made deals and gave people jobs to win votes and get things done in politics. The Panic of 1837 led to a less flattering nickname—Van Ruin.

William Henry Harrison

fact file

9th President
March–April 1841

Born: February 9, 1773, in Charles City County, VA

Wife: Anna Tuthill Symmes

Children: Elizabeth Bassett, John Cleves Symmes, Lucy Singleton, William Henry, John Scott, Mary Symmes, Carter Bassett, Anna Tuthill, James Findlay

Vice President: John Tyler

Political Party: Whig

Died: April 4, 1841, in Washington, DC

William Henry Harrison was the youngest of seven children. His parents were friends with George and Martha Washington, and Harrison's father signed the Declaration of Independence.

Young Harrison wanted to be an army officer, but his father wanted him to be a doctor. After his father died, Harrison left medical school to join the army. As an officer and politician in the Northwest Territories, Harrison negotiated with and sometimes fought Native Americans to clear the way for white settlers. He won a major battle against the Shawnee near a river called Tippecanoe, which earned him a famous nickname—Old Tippecanoe.

After the War of 1812, Harrison turned his attention to politics. He was a member of Congress and ran for president in 1836. He lost that election, but he didn't give up. In 1840, Harrison ran again and won.

Harrison took the oath of office on a cold, wet day in March. His speech lasted nearly two hours, and he didn't wear a coat or hat. Soon he had a cold, and then pneumonia. He died a month later. Today he's remembered for having the shortest term of any U.S. president.

★ Tippecanoe and Tyler Too!

Harrison's campaign slogan, which reminded voters that he was a war hero, was one of the most popular of all time. Harrison was Tippecanoe. Tyler was John Tyler, Harrison's choice for vice president.

★ Strange But True

Doctors tried to cure the president's pneumonia, but they probably did more harm than good. They put heated suction cups on Harrison's chest to draw out the sickness and drained some of his blood.

When everything else failed, they tried Native American cures. One included live snakes!

★ Funeral Procession

Harrison was the first president to die in office. Pallbearers escorted his body up Pennsylvania Avenue to the Capitol led by a riderless horse. Presidential funeral processions—or parades—follow the same route today.

John Tyler

fact file

10th President
1841–1845

Born: March 29, 1790, in Charles City County, VA

First Wife: Letitia Christian (died 1842); **Second Wife:** Julia Gardiner (married 1844)

Children: Mary, Robert, John, Letitia, Elizabeth, Anne Contesse, Alice, Tazewell, David Gardiner, John Alexander, Julia Gardiner, Lachlan, Lyon Gardiner, Robert Fitzwalter, Pearl

Vice President: None

Political Party: Whig

Died: January 18, 1862, in Richmond, VA

John Tyler was born on a Virginia tobacco plantation, which was worked by slaves. His father and Thomas Jefferson were good friends. Young Tyler, whose mother died when he was seven, went to local schools and then to the College of William and Mary. Afterward, he studied law in his father's office. When his father was elected governor of Virginia, Tyler moved to Richmond with him.

Tyler wanted to do more than be a lawyer. Soon he was involved in politics. By the time he became William Henry Harrison's vice president, Tyler had been a state legislator, the governor of Virginia, and a congressman.

When Harrison died, the Constitution wasn't clear about what would happen next. It said the vice president would take over as president, but would he be the decision maker, or would he simply carry out the wishes of Congress? Tyler insisted that he had the full powers of the presidency. He took the oath of office and moved into the White House in April 1841.

As president, his proslavery policies angered abolitionists. By the time he left office, the country was more divided than ever between those who were proslavery and those who were against it.

The Civil War began sixteen years after Tyler left office. The Confederate States of America elected Tyler to their new Congress, making him an enemy of the United States. He died before he could take office.

★ Sherwood Forest

Tyler thought of himself as a political outlaw, like Robin Hood. In 1842, he bought a plantation and named it Sherwood Forest, after the forest in the Robin Hood stories.

★ Children

Tyler had more children than any other president—fifteen! His last child was born when he was seventy years old.

★ Hail to the Chief

Julia Tyler, Tyler's second wife, started the tradition of playing "Hail to the Chief" when the president arrives at official gatherings.

James K. Polk

11th President
1845–1849

fact file

Born: November 2, 1795, in Mecklenburg County, NC

Wife: Sarah Childress

Children: None

Vice President: George M. Dallas

Political Party: Democrat

Died: June 15, 1849, in Nashville, TN

When **James K. Polk** was ten, his family made a long journey by wagon from North Carolina to Tennessee. The journey damaged his health, and Polk wasn't strong enough for frontier farming, but he was a good student. He graduated at the top of his class from the University of North Carolina.

After college, Polk became a lawyer and a politician. By the time he was nominated for president, he had served in Congress and as the governor of Tennessee.

When he was running for president, Polk promised to allow Texas to join the Union as a slave state. To win the approval of Northern voters, he suggested the country add Oregon as a free state. Polk believed in Manifest Destiny, or the idea that the borders of the United States should stretch from the Atlantic to the Pacific oceans.

To achieve that, Polk had to buy California from Mexico. Mexico refused to sell its land, so Polk started a war. Two years and many battles later, the United States won.

When Polk left office after one term, the country was much bigger, but also more divided over slavery than ever. He died three months after leaving office.

★ Young Hickory

Polk earned the nickname Young Hickory because of his friendship with Andrew Jackson. Like Jackson, he was born in the Carolinas and settled in Tennessee. He also supported Jackson's policies in Congress.

★ From Sea to Shining Sea

Polk was the first president of a United States that stretched from the Atlantic to the Pacific oceans. The Oregon Territory, acquired from Great Britain, became Washington, Oregon, Idaho, and parts of Montana and Wyoming. In addition to Texas, the land he took from Mexico became California, New Mexico, Arizona, Nevada, Utah, and parts of Colorado and Wyoming.

★ Thanksgiving

Sarah Polk hosted the first Thanksgiving dinner in the White House.

Zachary Taylor

12th President
1849–1850

fact file

Born: November 24, 1784, near Barboursville, VA

Wife: Margaret Mackall Smith

Children: Ann Mackall, Sarah Knox, Octavia Pannill, Margaret Smith, Mary Elizabeth, Richard

Vice President: Millard Fillmore

Political Party: Whig

Died: July 9, 1850, in Washington, DC

Zachary Taylor was born in Virginia and grew up on the Kentucky frontier. Young Taylor's handwriting, spelling, and grammar were not very good, but he wanted to go into the military, where such things didn't matter.

Instead of going to college, Taylor became an army officer. He fought in the War of 1812 and in battles for land against Native Americans. He also fought to protect Native American lands from white settlers. Taylor wore old farm clothes into battle and lived the same life as his soldiers, so they gave him the nickname Old Rough-and-Ready.

In the Mexican-American War, Taylor led his men to victory in important battles. People compared him to war heroes like George Washington and Andrew Jackson.

Taylor wasn't a politician, so he was surprised when the Whig party asked him to run for president. They thought the war hero would win the election, and he did.

Taylor was a slave owner, but he thought new states should decide for themselves whether they would be free or slave states. Some Southern states threatened to leave the United States if new free states entered the Union. Taylor was ready to go to war to keep the country together.

Then Taylor died suddenly. He celebrated July 4, 1850, at the Washington Monument. It was a hot day, and Taylor cooled off with a snack of cherries that probably had bacteria on them. He fell ill and died five days later.

★ Return to Sender

Taylor got so much mail as a war hero that he told the postmaster to return all the letters that came marked "postage due." At the time, mail didn't have to have a stamp if the person who received it was willing to pay. Taylor never got the letter telling him that he was nominated for president because he refused to pay the postage. Someone had to go in person to give him the news.

★ Presidential Pets

Old Whitey was Taylor's favorite warhorse. Taylor brought Old Whitey to Washington and let him graze on the White House lawn, but visitors kept pulling hairs from the horse's tail for souvenirs. Taylor finally had to put the horse in a stable to keep him safe.

Millard Fillmore

13th President
1850–1853

fact file

Born: January 7, 1800, in Summerhill, NY

First Wife: Abigail Powers (died 1853);
Second Wife: Caroline Carmichael McIntosh (married 1858)

Children: Millard Powers, Mary Abigail

Vice President: None

Political Party: Whig

Died: March 8, 1874, in Buffalo, NY

Millard Fillmore was born in a log cabin on a rocky farm in upstate New York. His family was very poor. Young Fillmore's farm chores kept him from going to school for more than a few months, but he was curious and wanted to learn.

His father arranged for Fillmore to learn a trade as a cloth maker. Fillmore hated the work and borrowed thirty dollars, a large amount of money at the time, to repay the cloth maker. Then he walked one hundred miles to the family farm. He worked hard, read every book he could get his hands on, and went to school.

Fillmore took a job with a judge, studied law, and married his teacher, Abigail Powers. Soon he was involved in New York State politics and was elected to the House of Representatives. When the Whigs needed a Northerner to balance Zachary Taylor's proslavery ideas in 1848, they asked Fillmore to run as vice president. Taylor and Fillmore won the election.

When Taylor died, Fillmore became president. Once he did, he worked quickly to prevent a civil war by supporting a series of agreements known as the Compromise of 1850.

The abolitionist Whigs were angry with Fillmore and chose a different candidate in the election of 1852. Fillmore retired to Buffalo, New York, but ran for president again in the 1856 election. He came in third.

★ Look It Up!

Fillmore was barely able to read when he used the little bit of money he had to buy a dictionary. When the cloth maker he worked for was busy, Fillmore would sneak peeks at the book to teach himself to read.

★ The Compromise of 1850

The Compromise of 1850 was really five separate deals.

- California was admitted to the Union as a free state.

- A border dispute between Texas and New Mexico was settled.

- New Mexico and Utah were named territories of the United States without clear rulings about slavery.

- The slave market in Washington, DC, was shut down.

- Federal law officers were required to return runaway slaves to their owners.

Franklin Pierce

14th President
1853–1857

fact file

Born: November 23, 1804, in Hillsborough, NH

Wife: Jane Means Appleton

Children: Franklin, Frank Robert, Benjamin

Vice President: William R. D. King

Political Party: Democrat

Died: October 8, 1869, in Concord, NH

Franklin Pierce grew up in rural New Hampshire. His parents wanted their eight children to have good educations. Pierce went to local schools until he was twelve, and then went away to continue his education. At fifteen, he started college in Maine, where he made lots of friends. His studies suffered, and in his first year, Pierce was last in his class. After that, he worked harder and graduated fifth in his class.

After college, Pierce became a lawyer and entered politics. His wife didn't like Washington, DC, so Pierce gave up national politics. But when the Democrats needed a candidate to run for president in 1852, they asked Pierce. They thought a Northerner who wasn't against slavery would be the best candidate. They were right. Pierce won.

When Pierce took office, the debate about slavery had settled down. The president stirred it up again when he undid part of the Missouri Compromise of 1820 that made slavery illegal in Kansas and Nebraska. Pierce said the citizens there should decide for themselves. Violent fighting broke out between proslavery and antislavery supporters in what came to be called Bleeding Kansas.

When Pierce left office, it seemed more and more likely that the two groups would force the country into a civil war.

★ Sad Times

Franklin and Jane Pierce had already lost two sons by the time Pierce ran for president. Their third son, Bennie, was killed in a train accident two months before Pierce took office.

★ Did You Know?

Pierce is the only president who did not use a Bible at his inauguration. He placed his hand on a law book instead.

★ Christmas Trees

Pierce was the first president to have a Christmas tree in the White House. Benjamin Harrison had the first official White House Christmas tree in 1889.

James Buchanan

fact file

15th President
1857–1861

Born: April 23, 1791, in Cove Gap, PA

Wife: Never married

Children: None

Vice President: John C. Breckinridge

Political Party: Democrat

Died: June 1, 1868, near Lancaster, PA

James Buchanan was the last president born in the eighteenth century. He was born in a log cabin and was the second of eleven children. His family was able to send him to good schools—although Buchanan was almost kicked out of college twice for misbehaving—and he graduated with honors. He went on to become a lawyer, but he put his career on hold during the War of 1812. Buchanan helped defend Baltimore after the British burned Washington, DC.

After the war, Buchanan served in the Pennsylvania legislature, the Congress, and was a diplomat in Russia and Great Britain as well as James K. Polk's secretary of state. What he really wanted to be was president. Buchanan tried to win his party's nomination in 1844, 1848, and 1852 before they finally said yes in 1856.

Buchanan took office just as the Supreme Court handed down an unpopular decision. A slave named Dred Scott had sued for his freedom because his owner brought him to live in a free state. The Court said Scott was property, not a citizen of the United States, and so he wasn't free.

Buchanan, who believed that individual states should have the right to make their own decisions about slavery, stood by the Court's decision. Northerners were angry. The South saw the decision as support of slavery. By the time Buchanan left office, the nation was on the brink of war.

★ Did You Know?

Buchanan was nearsighted in one eye and farsighted in the other. He had a habit of keeping one eye closed, depending on whether what he was looking at was far away or close up.

★ Harriet Lane

Buchanan was the only president who never married. His niece, Harriet Lane, was his hostess during his career. She traveled with him to England when he was minister to Great Britain, and acted as First Lady in the White House.

★ Slavery

Buchanan was personally against slavery. He sometimes bought slaves just to free them.

Abraham Lincoln

16th President
1861–1865

fact file

Born: February 12, 1809, in Hardin County, KY

Wife: Mary Todd

Children: Robert Todd, Edward Baker, William Wallace, Thomas (Tad)

Vice President: 1st term Hannibal Hamlin; 2nd term Andrew Johnson

Political Party: Republican

Died: April 15, 1865, in Washington, DC

Abraham Lincoln, who is often referred to as the United States' greatest president, was born in a one-room log cabin in Kentucky. Young Lincoln spent less than a year in pioneer schools, but he loved to learn. He walked miles to borrow books and read by firelight.

As a young man of 6 feet 4 inches, Lincoln stood out from the crowd. At twenty-five, he was elected to the Illinois legislature, and later to the U.S. House of Representatives.

In 1858, Lincoln ran for the Senate against one of the nation's most popular politicians, Stephen Douglas. Lincoln lost, but the debates between the two men brought Lincoln national attention. Two years later, Lincoln ran for president and won.

By the time Lincoln was inaugurated, seven states had left the Union to form the Confederate States of America. They believed that Lincoln, who was abolitionist, threatened their right to make their own decisions. Soon four more states joined them. Lincoln refused to let them leave the United States. The Civil War began six weeks after Lincoln took office. By the time it ended four years later, six hundred thousand Americans had died. The Union was preserved and slavery was abolished. President Lincoln led the nation through its worst moment in history.

On April 14, 1865, just five days after Southern general Robert E. Lee surrendered, an actor named John Wilkes Booth shot Lincoln. He died the next morning.

★ Odd Jobs

As a young man, Lincoln split logs into rails to build fences. Once, he traded rails for fabric to make pants. He also worked on a riverboat, ran a store, and was a surveyor and a postmaster before he taught himself to be a lawyer.

★ Emancipation Proclamation

Lincoln issued the Emancipation Proclamation in early 1863. The document freed the slaves in the Confederate states. By the end of the war, more than 180,000 black soldiers, many of them former slaves, served in the Union army.

★ Lincoln's Filing Cabinet

Lincoln stashed his mail, his bankbook, and important papers in his stovepipe hat.

Andrew Johnson

fact file

17th President
1865–1869

Born: December 29, 1808, in Raleigh, NC

Wife: Eliza McCardle

Children: Martha, Charles, Mary, Robert, Andrew

Vice President: None

Political Party: Democrat

Died: July 31, 1875, in Carter's Station, TN

Andrew Johnson grew up in greater poverty than any other president—even Abraham Lincoln. His parents could barely read and write, and his father died when he was three. Johnson never attended a day of school. When he was fourteen, his mother apprenticed him to a tailor. People read aloud to him while he worked, and Johnson taught himself to read. Later, his wife taught him writing and arithmetic.

Johnson grew up believing that the states should be able to make their own decisions about slavery. He also believed that leaving the Union was wrong. He was the only Southern senator who stayed loyal to the Union during the Civil War. The Southern states called him a traitor, but he was a hero in the North. Lincoln asked Johnson to be his vice president for his second term.

After President Lincoln's death, Johnson became president. He had the hard job of trying to put the country back together. He let the South decide how to treat the newly freed slaves, which made Northerners angry. Johnson and Congress fought at every turn. Congress passed laws he disagreed with.

In 1868, Congress impeached President Johnson, which means they said he broke the law. There was a trial to remove him from office, but Johnson was found not guilty by one vote.

★ Fourteenth Amendment

Johnson did not want former slaves to have the same legal rights as white people. Congress disagreed. In 1866, Congress passed the Fourteenth Amendment to the Constitution, making former slaves full citizens of the United States.

★ Did You Know?

Johnson asked to be buried wrapped in a U.S. flag, with a copy of the Constitution under his head.

★ Medal of Honor

Johnson awarded the Congressional Medal of Honor to the first and only woman (Dr. Mary Edwards Walker) in 1865.

Ulysses S. Grant

fact file

18th President
1869–1877

Born: April 27, 1822, in Point Pleasant, OH

Wife: Julia Boggs Dent

Children: Frederick Dent, Ulysses Simpson, Ellen Wrenshall, Jesse Root

Vice President: 1st term Schuyler Colfax; 2nd term Henry Wilson

Political Party: Republican

Died: July 23, 1885, in Mount McGregor, NY

Hiram Ulysses Grant was called Ulysses by his parents and his five younger brothers and sisters. His father was a tanner—a dirty, smelly job. Young Grant helped out, but he hated the work. He found school boring, too, but the shy boy was an expert horseman. People from miles around brought him their horses to train.

When Grant was first accepted into the United States Military Academy at West Point, he didn't want to go. Then he realized it was his chance to travel and go to college. He impressed his classmates with his horsemanship, and fought in the Mexican-American War under Zachary Taylor.

After the war, Grant married and tried a number of professions, including farming and working in the real estate business. He failed at most of them. When the Civil War started, he joined the army again and led troops in many successful battles. President Lincoln asked Grant to be in charge of the entire Union army. On April 9, 1865, Confederate General Robert E. Lee surrendered to Grant. The Civil War was over.

Grant was a hero, and voters were happy to elect him president. He was a better general than he was a president. Even though Grant himself was honest, some of his political friends were not. There were many scandals during his second term.

★ What's in a Name?

When Grant's congressman wrote him a letter of recommendation to West Point, he mistakenly wrote Grant's name as *Ulysses S. Grant* instead of *Hiram Ulysses Grant*. Grant tried to correct the mistake, but the S stayed. His West Point classmates nicknamed him Uncle Sam.

★ Yellowstone

Under Grant's leadership, the country established its first national park—Yellowstone.

★ Whoa!

President Grant was once stopped for speeding in Washington, DC. The police officer took away his horse and carriage, and Grant had to walk the rest of the way home to the White House. He paid a twenty-dollar speeding ticket.

Rutherford B. Hayes

19th President
1877–1881

fact file

Born: October 4, 1822, in Delaware, OH

Wife: Lucy Ware Webb

Children: Birchard Austin, James Webb Cook, Rutherford Platt, Joseph Thompson, George Crook, Fanny, Scott Russell, Manning Force

Vice President: William A. Wheeler

Political Party: Republican

Died: January 17, 1893, in Fremont, OH

Rutherford B. Hayes was born ten weeks after his father died. Hayes was often sick as a baby, and wasn't allowed to play outside until he was seven. He and his sister, Fanny, became great friends during that time.

He wasn't strong, but young Hayes, nicknamed Ruddy, was an excellent student and graduated first in his class from college. He went to Harvard Law School and opened a law practice in Ohio. By the time he was nominated for president, Hayes had fought in the Civil War, been a congressman, and served as governor of Ohio.

On the night of the election, Hayes thought he had lost. His opponent had more popular votes, but Hayes had more electoral votes. There were also questions about illegal voting in some southern states.

For weeks, no one knew who won. Congress named a special committee to decide. They said that Hayes won the election by one vote. Many people were angry about the outcome.

Hayes's first official duty was to take the oath of office, which he did secretly in the Red Room of the White House. Two days later, he was sworn in again in a public ceremony.

As president, Hayes gave Southern states more say in their government. Unfortunately, they passed laws that took rights away from former slaves. Hayes retired after one term, but he spoke out for equal education for African American children for the rest of his life.

★ Hello?

Hayes was the first president to have a telephone in the White House. The inventor of the telephone, Alexander Graham Bell, installed it and gave it the phone number 1.

★ Easter Eggs

President and Mrs. Hayes held the first Easter Egg Roll on the White House lawn in 1878. Now it's a yearly tradition.

★ Presidential Pets

Hayes and his wife brought a lot of animals to the White House. They had Jersey cows, the first Siamese kitten in the United States, two shepherd dogs, one goat, four canaries, two hunting pups, and one spaniel named Duke. They also had four other kittens, a mockingbird, and several horses.

James A. Garfield

20th President
March–September 1881

fact file

Born: November 19, 1831, in Orange Township, OH

Wife: Lucretia Rudolph

Children: Eliza Arabella, Harry Augustus, James Rudolph, Mary, Irvin McDowell, Abram, Edward

Vice President: Chester A. Arthur

Political Party: Republican

Died: September 19, 1881, in Elberon, NJ

James A. Garfield was the last of the presidents to be born in a log cabin. His father died when he was a baby, and young Garfield had to work on the family farm. He loved the outdoors, but he didn't want to be a farmer. He wanted to go to college, and so he worked as a farmhand, a carpenter, and a part-time teacher to support his mother and pay for school. After college, Garfield became a college professor, married, and studied law.

Garfield was serving in the Ohio Senate when the Civil War broke out. He joined the Union army and led his men to victory in a battle in Kentucky. He was still with the army when he was elected to the U.S. House of Representatives. Garfield thought he should stay with the army, but President Lincoln asked him to go to Washington to join the House. In 1880, he ran for president.

Garfield promised to clean up dishonesty in government. He didn't think people should get good jobs in politics just because they were friends of the president. One of those people was angry when Garfield refused to give him a job. He shot the president, and Garfield died eleven weeks later.

★ Man Overboard

When he was sixteen, Garfield ran away to work on the canal boats that ran between Ohio and Pennsylvania. In six weeks he fell overboard fourteen times! He caught a bad fever and had to go home.

★ Who Killed the President?

A mentally disturbed man shot Garfield in the back. But the bullet didn't kill him. Doctors tried to find the bullet using a new machine invented by Alexander Graham Bell. All of the dirty instruments used to remove the bullet led to the blood poisoning that really killed the president.

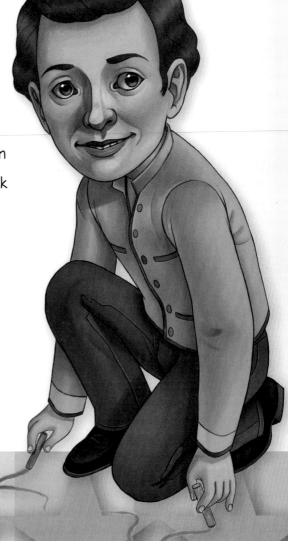

★ Strange But True

Garfield could write with both hands (ambidextrous). Sometimes he would entertain people by writing Latin with one hand and Greek with the other—at the same time!

Chester A. Arthur

21st President
1881–1885

fact file

Born: October 5, 1829, in Fairfield, VT

Wife: Ellen Lewis Herndon

Children: William Lewis Herndon, Chester Alan, Ellen Herndon

Vice President: None

Political Party: Republican

Died: November 18, 1886, in New York, NY

Chester A. Arthur was never elected to anything before he became vice president. The world was shocked when President Garfield died and Arthur took over.

Arthur's father was a minister and the family moved a lot from one church to another in Vermont and New York. He learned to read and write before he started school and was a good student.

In college, Arthur was known for playing pranks, but he graduated in the top third of his class. He taught school to help pay his tuition. Later he became a lawyer with one of the top firms in New York City and made his name fighting for rights for African Americans.

During the Civil War, Arthur was responsible for making sure New York's soldiers had uniforms and supplies. Afterward, the Republican Party gave him a powerful job collecting import duties, or taxes, from ships that sailed into the Port of New York. Arthur then gave jobs and raises to the people who supported the party's candidates with votes and money.

Arthur was shocked that someone who wanted one of those jobs would kill a president. As president, he surprised everyone by doing away with that dishonest system and making sure that people were given jobs and raises based on their abilities.

★ Civil Rights

More than one hundred years before Rosa Parks refused to give up her seat on a bus in Alabama, Arthur defended a similar case in New York City in 1854. Elizabeth Jennings was thrown off a "whites only" horse-drawn streetcar. Arthur sued the streetcar company and won $225 from the company for Jennings. From then on, black passengers were able to sit wherever they wanted on New York City streetcars.

★ Elegant Arthur

The press nicknamed the president Elegant Arthur because he liked nice clothes and had a lot of them—including eighty pairs of pants! He thought the White House was shabby and wouldn't move in until it had a complete makeover.

★ A Rose for Ellen

Arthur's wife, Ellen Lewis Herndon, died before he became president. In the White House, he had a fresh rose placed by her picture every day.

Grover Cleveland

22nd President
24th President
1885–1889/1893–1897

fact file

Born: March 18, 1837, in Caldwell, NJ

Wife: Frances Folsom

Children: Ruth, Esther, Marion, Richard Folsom, Francis Grover

Vice President: 1st term Thomas A. Hendricks; 2nd term Adlai E. Stevenson

Political Party: Democrat

Died: June 24, 1908, in Princeton, NJ

Grover Cleveland is the only president to serve two terms separated by another president. In 1888, he lost the election to Benjamin Harrison. In their 1892 rematch, Cleveland took the White House back.

Cleveland had eight brothers and sisters. His father was a minister, and the family moved from New Jersey to upstate New York when he was young. He was sixteen when his father died, and Cleveland quit school to go to work, studying law part-time.

Cleveland had served as a county sheriff, but he was surprised when the local Democrats asked him to run for mayor of Buffalo in 1881. He won and worked hard to clean up corruption. Soon he was governor of New York, and three years after he became mayor, he was elected president.

Cleveland worked hard—he was often at his desk until three o'clock in the morning—but his many vetoes made even members of his own political party angry. In 1888, Harrison won the election. Cleveland promised he would be back, and four years later he was.

At the beginning of his second term, the United States entered difficult economic times. Businesses failed and people couldn't find jobs. Many people thought Cleveland didn't do enough to turn things around. By the end of his second term, the American people were ready for a change.

★ White House Wedding

Cleveland married Frances Folsom in 1886. It was the first and only time a president got married in the White House.

★ Statue of Liberty

Lady Liberty was shipped to her permanent home in New York Harbor during President Cleveland's first term. He dedicated the statue in October 1886 in front of thousands of spectators.

★ Secret Surgery

President Cleveland was diagnosed with mouth cancer in 1893. He didn't want to worry the American people, so he had a secret operation on a friend's yacht. Part of his jaw was replaced with rubber, but the doctors left no scars. The secret didn't get out for many years.

Benjamin Harrison

23rd President
1889–1893

fact file

Born: August 20, 1833, in North Bend, OH

First Wife: Caroline Lavinia Scott (died 1892); **Second Wife:** Mary Scott Lord Dimmick (married 1896)

Children: Russell Benjamin, Mary Scott, Elizabeth

Vice President: Levi P. Morton

Political Party: Republican

Died: March 13, 1901, in Indianapolis, IN

Benjamin Harrison was a little boy on an Ohio farm when his grandfather, William Henry Harrison, became president. As a child, Harrison hunted, fished, chopped wood, and took care of the farm animals. He also liked to sneak away from his seven brothers and sisters to read in his grandfather's library. Like his grandfather, Harrison studied law. During the Civil War, he became a brigadier general and fought for the Union. Afterward he settled in Indianapolis and was elected senator. Harrison fought for rights for Native Americans and Civil War veterans.

Six new states joined the Union during Harrison's term in office—more than in any other presidency. He worked to pass the Sherman Antitrust Act, a law to protect people from big companies' high prices.

By the end of Harrison's term, Americans were growing concerned about the taxes they had to pay on goods from other countries. Former president

Cleveland promised to lower those taxes when he ran against Harrison in 1892. This time, Cleveland won. Harrison retired to Indianapolis and started his law practice again. He died nine years later.

★ Little Ben

Because Harrison was only 5 feet 6 inches tall, Democrats called him Little Ben. Republicans answered by saying that he was big enough to wear the hat of his grandfather, Old Tippecanoe.

★ Front Porch Campaign

Harrison ran for president with what was called a front porch campaign. He stayed at home in Indianapolis and had political talks with citizens and reporters who were encouraged to visit.

★ Is It Cold in Here?

Harrison was so stiff and formal in his dealings with people that his White House staff secretly called him the Human Iceberg.

★ Did You Know?

Benjamin Harrison was the first president to have electricity in the White House. First Lady Caroline Lavinia Harrison was afraid the light switches would shock her, so she never turned them on.

William McKinley

25th President
1897–1901

fact file

Born: January 29, 1843, in Niles, OH

Wife: Ida Saxton

Children: Katherine, Ida

Vice President: 1st term Garret A. Hobart; 2nd term Theodore Roosevelt

Political Party: Republican

Died: September 14, 1901, in Buffalo, NY

William McKinley was born in a small town in Ohio. He had seven brothers and sisters and spent his free time fishing, hunting, ice-skating, horseback riding, and swimming. He liked school and studied hard. He couldn't afford to finish college, but he was a brave soldier during the Civil War and was promoted many times. He served on the staff of Colonel Rutherford B. Hayes, another future president of the United States.

When the war ended, McKinley studied law and began his political career. By the time he ran for president in 1896, he had been a congressman and the governor of Ohio.

When McKinley took office, Cuba was at war with Spain for independence. Many Americans were on Cuba's side. On February 15, 1898, the battleship USS *Maine* blew up and sank off the coast of Havana. No one knew what caused the explosion, but the American people blamed Spain. The U.S. blocked Cuba's ports, Spain declared war on the U.S., and Congress declared war on Spain. The Spanish-American War ended in an American victory in only one hundred days.

In 1900, McKinley easily won reelection with Theodore Roosevelt as vice president at his side. Six months into his second term, an anarchist fired two shots at the president in Buffalo, New York. McKinley died on September 14, 1901.

★ Civil War Service

McKinley volunteered for the Union army when he was a teenager. His first job was to bring hot food and coffee to the troops on the front lines.

★ World Power

At the end of the Spanish-American War, Cuba won its independence and the United States gained the territories of Puerto Rico, Guam, and the Philippines. The United States was building an empire and had become one of the world's colonial powers.

★ Did You Know?

After he was shot, the president was rushed to the hospital in an ambulance. It was the first time a president had taken a ride in a new invention called the automobile.

Theodore Roosevelt

26th President
1901–1909

fact file

Born: October 27, 1858, in New York, NY

First Wife: Alice Hathaway Lee (died 1884); **Second Wife:** Edith Kermit Carow (married 1886)

Children: Alice Lee, Theodore, Kermit, Ethel Carow, Archibald Bulloch, Quentin

Vice President: Charles W. Fairbanks

Political Party: Republican

Died: January 6, 1919, in Oyster Bay, NY

Theodore Roosevelt, known as Teddy, had asthma as a child and was often sick. His father believed that exercise was a great cure, and young Roosevelt spent lots of time outdoors. By the time he went to Harvard, Roosevelt was strong enough to join the boxing team.

After graduation, Roosevelt entered New York politics. Then his wife and his mother died on the same day in 1884. Roosevelt was heartbroken. He moved to North Dakota and taught himself to be a cowboy and a rancher. Two years later, he moved back to New York, remarried, and became the head of New York City's police department in 1895.

When the Spanish-American War broke out, Roosevelt organized a volunteer army. He came home a war hero. Soon afterward, he was elected governor of New York and then vice president. When President McKinley died, Roosevelt became the youngest president ever, at forty-two.

Roosevelt started building the Panama Canal to connect the Atlantic and Pacific oceans, and he won the Nobel Peace Prize for helping end a war between Japan and Russia in 1905. His love of the outdoors led him to create five national parks, eighteen national monuments, and fifty-one wildlife refuges.

After he left office, Roosevelt went on safari in Africa and sent hundreds of animals back to the Smithsonian Institution. He died in his sleep in 1919.

★ The Teddy Bear

In November 1902, Roosevelt went on a bear hunt. His guide found a small bear and tied it to a tree. Roosevelt said it would be wrong to shoot the animal. The story may have led a toy maker in Brooklyn to create a stuffed bear he named Teddy's Bear. The teddy bear has been a popular toy ever since.

★ Rough Riders

Roosevelt's volunteer army was made up of cowboys, Native Americans, college athletes, and New York City policemen. He called them the Rough Riders and led them on a famous charge in the battle of San Juan, Cuba.

★ Presidential Pets

The Roosevelts had more than forty pets when they lived in the White House. These included birds, guinea pigs, a badger, a pony, a one-legged rooster, a pig, a raccoon, cats, dogs, and rats. The children also liked snakes. Alice Roosevelt liked to wear a snake named Emily Spinach around her neck to shock people.

William Howard Taft

27th President
1909–1913

fact file

Born: September 15, 1857, in Cincinnati, OH

Wife: Helen Herron

Children: Robert Alphonso, Helen Herron, Charles Phelps

Vice President: James S. Sherman

Political Party: Republican

Died: March 8, 1930, in Washington, DC

William Howard Taft loved sports, especially baseball, during his childhood in Ohio. He was a good second baseman and a power hitter. He was also a good student and graduated second in his high school class. At Yale, he graduated second in his class again and went on to law school. Afterward he started a law practice and worked as a judge.

President McKinley asked Taft to be governor of the Philippine Islands, and when President Roosevelt needed a man to be in charge of the Panama Canal, he also turned to Taft. Taft wanted nothing more than to be a judge, but he felt he had to take on these jobs. When President Roosevelt asked Taft to run for president, his wife talked him into saying yes.

Taft won the election, but he disappointed the Republican Party by not being as bold and decisive as Roosevelt had been. In the election of 1912, Roosevelt ran against his former friend for a new party called the Progressive Party. Taft and Roosevelt split the Republican vote and Democrat Woodrow Wilson won the election.

In 1921, Taft finally got the job he always wanted. President Warren G. Harding named him the chief justice of the Supreme Court of the United States.

★ Big Bill

"Big Bill" Taft weighed 332 pounds and was the biggest president ever. He got stuck in the White House bathtub and had to have a custom-made tub installed. It was big enough for four average-size men.

★ Presidential Pets

President Taft liked fresh milk. His pet cow, Pauline Wayne, grazed on the White House lawn. Every day, her milk was on the president's table.

★ Forty-eight States

When New Mexico and Arizona joined the Union in 1912, Taft became the first president of forty-eight states.

★ Play Ball!

President Taft was a big baseball fan. He was the first president to throw the first pitch at a game on opening day.

Woodrow Wilson

28th President
1913–1921

fact file

Born: December 28, 1856, in Staunton, VA

First Wife: Ellen Louise Axson (died 1914); **Second Wife:** Edith Bolling Galt (married 1915)

Children: Margaret Woodrow, Jessie Woodrow, Eleanor Randolph

Vice President: Thomas R. Marshall

Political Party: Democrat

Died: February 3, 1924, Washington, DC

Woodrow Wilson was born in Virginia. His first memory was hearing that Abraham Lincoln had been elected president. He grew up in Georgia and South Carolina, surrounded by soldiers. During the war, he studied at home with his father. Later he went to Princeton and Johns Hopkins Universities. He became a college professor and was the president of Princeton when he was asked to run for governor of New Jersey. Wilson won, and soon had a national reputation. In 1912, the Democrats asked him to run for president.

Wilson was elected during a difficult time. He reformed the banking system, fought for an eight-hour day for workers, and supported laws against child labor. His biggest challenge came in 1914, when World War I broke out in Europe. Wilson tried to keep the United States out of the war. Then German submarines sank American ships. On April 6, 1917, the United States declared war on Germany.

When the war ended, Wilson tried to create the League of Nations, which would solve problems with words instead of weapons. He won the Nobel Peace Prize for his work, but Congress didn't support his plan. Without the United States, the League could not succeed.

Wilson left office feeling like a failure, but he is remembered as one of the United States' greatest presidents.

★ Dyslexia

Wilson had dyslexia, a learning disorder that made it hard for him to learn reading, writing, and math.

★ Women's Suffrage

The National Women's Party put pressure on President Wilson to help women win the right to vote. Before the end of his second term in 1920, Congress passed the Nineteenth Amendment, giving women the right to vote.

★ Counting Sheep

President and Mrs. Wilson brought a flock of sheep to the White House after the United States entered the war. The sheep "mowed" the lawn, saving gas and labor. Their wool was sold to earn money for the Red Cross and for war hospitals.

Warren G. Harding

29th President
1921–1923

fact file

Born: November 2, 1865, in Corsica, OH

Wife: Florence Kling DeWolfe

Children: None

Vice President: Calvin Coolidge

Political Party: Republican

Died: August 2, 1923, in San Francisco, CA

Warren G. Harding grew up in Ohio, where he went to a one-room schoolhouse, swam in a nearby creek, and played in the village band. When he was fourteen, he started college. Afterward, he tried many jobs. He was a teacher, an insurance salesman, and a newspaper reporter. Then he raised enough money to buy his own newspaper.

Once the paper was successful, he entered politics. As a senator, he skipped more votes than he showed up for. He never did anything important and he made more friends than enemies. Harding wasn't the Republican Party's first choice to run for president in 1920. He was chosen because they couldn't decide between the top two candidates. Harding himself was shocked when he was nominated.

As president, Harding was known more for his golf and poker games than he was for his work. He thought Congress should make most of the decisions.

Hints of illegal behavior among his inner circle began to trouble Harding.

When the American people learned that some of the men who worked closely with the president were taking bribes, his health was already weak. After this news, Harding died suddenly. Even though he did not do anything illegal himself, Harding's short presidency is considered one of the worst in history.

★ The Poker Cabinet

While he was president, Harding played poker with his advisors twice a week. People started calling them the Poker Cabinet.

★ The Teapot Dome Scandal

The biggest scandal of Harding's administration—the Teapot Dome affair—didn't fully come to light until after his death. One of Harding's cabinet members took illegal payments in exchange for oil-drilling rights on federal lands near Teapot Dome, Wyoming.

★ Presidential Papers

After President Harding died, his wife destroyed most of his personal papers and his letters. She was trying to avoid more gossip and scandal.

★ Big Foot

Harding had the biggest feet of any president—size 14!

Calvin Coolidge

30th President
1923–1929

fact file

Born: July 4, 1872, in Plymouth Notch, VT

Wife: Grace Anna Goodhue

Children: John, Calvin

Vice President: 1st term none; 2nd term Charles G. Dawes

Political Party: Republican

Died: January 5, 1933, in Northampton, MA

Calvin Coolidge became president unexpectedly in the middle of the night when President Harding died. Coolidge worked hard to restore trust in the government. He fired dishonest staff members and brought a plain, honest, and direct style to the White House.

Coolidge grew up in a cottage attached to the post office and general store owned by his father in rural Vermont. He learned to drive oxen and plow the land, and one of his favorite activities was making maple syrup. He went to college and became a lawyer. Then he climbed the political ladder all the way from city councilman to governor of Massachusetts and then to vice president.

The 1920s were good years for American businesses and Coolidge was a popular fill-in president. In 1924, he ran for president himself and won with the slogan "Keep Cool With Coolidge."

By the end of the 1920s, farmers were struggling and banks were shutting down. Coolidge supported big business rather than working people. A few months after he left office, the stock market crashed, and the country entered the Great Depression.

★ Presidential Pets

Many people sent animal gifts to President Coolidge. He received a bear from Mexico, a hippo from South Africa, and a wallaby from Australia. Most of the animals were sent to the zoo, but the president took a liking to a raccoon. He named her Rebecca and let her roam the White House.

★ Strange But True

Coolidge received a mechanical horse as a gift when he was in the White House. He liked to ride it for exercise, wearing a cowboy hat.

★ Silent Cal

Coolidge didn't talk much. In fact, he said so little that people gave him the nickname Silent Cal. Once, a dinner guest at the White House told Coolidge she had made a bet that she could get him to say three words. Silent Cal said, "You lose."

Herbert Hoover

31st President
1929–1933

fact file

Born: August 10, 1874, in West Branch, IA

Wife: Lou Henry

Children: Herbert Clark, Allan Henry

Vice President: Charles Curtis

Political Party: Republican

Died: October 20, 1964, in New York, NY

Just seven months after **Herbert Hoover** took office, the stock market crashed and the country entered the Great Depression. Times were harder than they had ever been.

Hoover was no stranger to hard times. He was an orphan at the age of nine. He was passed from relative to relative, and finally ended up with an uncle in Oregon. Hoover was a bad student and he barely passed the exams for college. He went to Stanford University and studied geology. Then he made his fortune traveling the world as a gold mine expert.

When World War I began, many Americans were trapped in Europe. Hoover, who was in London, helped 120,000 of them get home. Later he raised millions of dollars for food and medicine for the war's European victims. He helped people in more than twenty countries.

After the war, Hoover entered politics. He won the 1928 election with the slogan "A chicken in every pot and a car in every garage." Then the stock market crashed, which meant the value of stocks suddenly dropped. Many stock owners were left poor. The good times were over.

Hoover tried to turn things around, but his programs failed. Americans thought he didn't care about their problems. Four years later, he ran for a second term and lost the election to Franklin Delano Roosevelt.

★ The Great Depression

The stock market crash in October 1929 led to the Great Depression. One-quarter of all workers couldn't find jobs, banks shut down, farms failed, and more than a million people were homeless. Many of them lived in towns of shacks they called Hoovervilles.

★ Hoover Dam

The Hoover Dam, named after President Hoover, is still considered a wonder of engineering. The dam stands across the Colorado River and distributes water to Arizona, California, Colorado, Nevada, New Mexico, Utah, and Wyoming.

★ Strange But True

Hoover liked to exercise with a medicine ball—a very heavy ball meant to build strength. His advisors had to join him for early morning games of catch followed by breakfast.

Franklin D. Roosevelt

fact file

32nd President
1933–1945

Born: January 30, 1882, in Hyde Park, NY

Wife: Anna Eleanor Roosevelt

Children: Anna Eleanor, James, Elliott, Franklin Delano Jr., John Aspinwall, one son who died in infancy

Vice President: 1st and 2nd terms John Nance Garner; 3rd term Henry Agard Wallace; 4th term Harry S. Truman

Political Party: Democrat

Died: April 12, 1945, in Warm Springs, GA

Franklin D. Roosevelt (FDR) led the country out of the Great Depression and saw it through the darkest days of World War II.

FDR was from a wealthy New York family. When he was a teenager, he went to boarding school and followed the career of a distant cousin—Theodore Roosevelt.

He went on to Harvard University and met another distant cousin, named Eleanor Roosevelt. They were married while FDR was at Columbia Law School. He began a political career, but was suddenly struck with a disease called polio. Within two days, he couldn't walk. FDR used a wheelchair for the rest of his life. Within three years, he was practicing law again, and then became governor of New York.

When he ran for president in 1932, FDR promised a New Deal for the American people, which included help for farmers and better working conditions for most Americans. Roosevelt also restored confidence in banks. He was reelected in 1936 and in 1940.

By 1940, the world was at war. Roosevelt tried to keep the United States out of it, but when Japan bombed naval bases at Pearl Harbor, the United States declared war on Japan. Germany and Italy declared war on the United States. FDR was a strong wartime leader, and when he ran for a fourth term, the American people voted for him again.

Shortly into his fourth term, FDR died of a stroke. One month later, the Allies, which included the United States, won the war in Europe.

★ Did You Know?

Roosevelt was the only president to serve more than two terms. He was elected *four* times! In 1951, Congress passed the Twenty-second Amendment to the Constitution, which set a limit of two terms.

★ Eleanor Roosevelt

Eleanor Roosevelt was one of the most popular First Ladies of all time. She often traveled for her husband, gave speeches and radio broadcasts, and spoke out in favor of her own causes. She wanted to make sure that all Americans, including African Americans, women, and immigrants, were a part of the New Deal.

Harry S. Truman

33rd President
1945–1953

fact file

Born: May 8, 1884, in Lamar, MO

Wife: Elizabeth (Bess) Virginia Wallace

Children: Mary Margaret

Vice President: 1st term none; 2nd term Alben W. Barkley

Political Party: Democratic

Died: December 26, 1972, in Kansas City, MO

Harry S. Truman became president on April 12, 1945, when President Roosevelt died. He was as shocked as the American people. "I felt like the moon, the stars, and all the planets had fallen on me," he said.

Truman was no stranger to hard times. His thick glasses made it difficult for him to play sports. Children teased him, but he spent his time reading every single book in the public library. His family couldn't afford college, and Truman worked many jobs before entering politics. He was a senator when FDR talked him into running for vice president in 1944.

The war in Europe ended soon after Truman became president, but the war with Japan raged on until August. Truman made the hard decision to drop two atomic bombs on two Japanese cities. Hundreds of thousands of people were killed, but Japan surrendered.

When the war ended, Truman helped start the United Nations. Then more problems arose in the world. The Cold War began between democratic and

Communist nations. Truman sent soldiers to South Korea to help the people in their war with Communist North Korea.

At home, Truman tried to continue FDR's work and created his own Fair Deal. Congress didn't support his policies, and he left office without achieving what he wanted to. Today he is remembered for strong leadership in tough times.

★ Bathtub Secrets

The glass carver who designed President Truman's bathtub hid a message in the glass, which read: "In this tub bathes the man whose heart is always clean and serves his people truthfully."

★ "The Buck Stops Here"

President Truman had a sign with this famous quotation on his desk. It meant that Truman couldn't "pass the buck." He was in charge and couldn't pass his responsibilities or the blame on to anyone else.

★ The Cold War

Communist government controls its citizens, industries, and finances. In a democracy, the people are in charge and have more freedoms. Truman wanted to keep the Soviet Union from spreading communism around the world. It was called a cold war because there were no actual battles even though the two countries were unfriendly to each other.

Dwight D. Eisenhower

34th President
1953–1961

fact file

Born: October 14, 1890, in Denison, TX

Wife: Mary (Mamie) Geneva Doud

Children: Doud Dwight, John Sheldon Doud

Vice President: Richard M. Nixon

Political Party: Republican

Died: March 28, 1969, in Washington, DC

Dwight D. Eisenhower grew up in a small farm town in Kansas, where he played and fought with his six brothers. He liked hunting, fishing, and football, and he loved military history. In 1911, he went to the military academy at West Point. He was a prankster and his teachers didn't think he would be a great officer.

Eisenhower proved them wrong. In the army, he was promoted many times. During World War II, he was put in charge of all the troops in Europe and led them to victory. He came home a hero. Both political parties asked him to run for president. At first, Eisenhower said no. In 1952, he agreed to run as a Republican.

As president, Eisenhower helped end the fighting between North and South Korea. He also tried to ease the Cold War troubles with the Soviet Union. At home, most Americans were happy, but African Americans were not being treated fairly. The Supreme Court ruled that segregated schools—schools that separated black students from white students—were illegal. Eisenhower sent federal troops to a high school in Little Rock, Arkansas, to protect African American children.

He retired after two terms to a farm in Gettysburg, Pennsylvania.

★ Camp David

The National Park Service found a spot for a presidential retreat near Washington, DC, in 1942. FDR named it Shangri-la, but Eisenhower thought the name was too fancy. He decided to rename the camp after his grandson, David. Presidents still go to Camp David to relax today.

★ Hall of Fame

Eisenhower loved to play golf. He made the game so popular that the number of Americans who played doubled while he was in office. In 2009, he was elected to the World Golf Hall of Fame.

★ Ike is Nifty!

Americans were encouraged to chant, "We like Ike!" during the 1952 election. By the end of his time in office, they were chanting, "Ike is nifty, Ike is nifty; started out with forty-eight; ended up with fifty." Alaska and Hawaii joined the Union during his presidency.

John F. Kennedy

35th President
1961–1963

fact file

Born: May 29, 1917, in Brookline, MA

Wife: Jacqueline Lee Bouvier

Children: Caroline Bouvier, John Fitzgerald Jr., Patrick Bouvier

Vice President: Lyndon Johnson

Political Party: Democrat

Died: November 22, 1963, in Dallas, TX

John F. Kennedy (JFK) grew up in a wealthy family surrounded by eight brothers and sisters. Young Kennedy was often sick. He nearly died of scarlet fever when he was two. But he was also athletic and smart. He graduated from Harvard with honors.

JFK's father wanted one of his sons to be the first Catholic president. When JFK's older brother, Joseph, died in World War II, his father's hopes fell on JFK's shoulders. He became a congressman and then a senator, and in 1960 he ran for president against Richard Nixon. Their debates were the first ever shown on television.

When JFK was president, the Cold War heated up. The United States tried to overthrow Cuba's Communist government. The mission was an embarrassing failure. Then the Soviet Union set up missiles in Cuba. Kennedy threatened to go to war if they weren't removed. The Soviet Union backed down.

At home, JFK fought for equal rights for all races and promised to send men to the moon and back. He also started the Peace Corps to help people in poor nations.

On November 22, 1963, JFK and his wife were riding in an open car in Dallas, Texas, when the president was shot. He died that same day. His calls for peace and justice continue to inspire Americans today.

★ War Hero

JFK became a World War II hero when a Japanese warship destroyed the boat under his command. JFK swam for four miles, some of them with the strap of one injured man's life vest in his teeth. He led all the survivors to safety.

★ Jackie Kennedy

First Lady Jackie Kennedy brought glamour to the White House. Women all over the world wanted to dress and style their hair as Jackie did. She restored the White House to make it a showcase of American history.

★ Who Shot JFK?

A gunman named Lee Harvey Oswald was charged with JFK's death. Oswald was murdered himself before he could stand trial. Government investigators agreed that Oswald was the only shooter, but some people continue to believe that Oswald had help.

Lyndon B. Johnson

fact file

43rd President
1963–1969

Born: August 27, 1908, near Stonewall, TX

Wife: Claudia Alta (Lady Bird) Taylor

Children: Lynda Bird, Luci Baines

Vice President: 1st term none; 2nd term Hubert H. Humphrey

Political Party: Democrat

Died: January 22, 1973, near Stonewall, TX

Lyndon B. Johnson (LBJ) was sworn in as president just two hours after the assassination of JFK. LBJ worked with Congress to pass laws inspired by JFK and his own War on Poverty.

LBJ had grown up in poverty. His childhood home didn't have electricity or indoor plumbing, and his high school was a three-mile mule ride way. Still, LBJ graduated president of his six-student class and became a teacher. His students were as poor as he was, and LBJ entered politics to make their lives better.

Before he was president, LBJ was a leader in the Senate. As president, he worked with Congress to pass bills that would improve lives. He got money for education and started a health care program for senior citizens. He easily won reelection in 1964.

The United States had big problems during LBJ's second term. African Americans didn't think he was doing enough for civil rights. Riots broke out in

American cities. The country was divided over a war in Vietnam. (American troops were helping the South Vietnamese fight against the Communist North Vietnamese.) Many Americans didn't think the United States should be fighting there.

LBJ decided not to run in 1968. He wanted to spend his time seeking peace, but he died before the Vietnam War ended.

★ Presidential Firsts

LBJ appointed the first African American to the Supreme Court, Thurgood Marshall, in 1967. Marshall was the great-grandson of a slave.

★ Civil Rights

Under LBJ, Congress passed the Civil Rights Act and the Voting Rights Act—laws that ended segregation and made sure that African Americans and other minorities had the right to vote.

★ LBJ

Lyndon B. and Lady Bird Johnson named their daughters Lynda Bird and Luci Baines so that all four members of the family would have the initials *LBJ*.

Richard M. Nixon

37th President
1969–1974

fact file

Born: January 9, 1913, in Yorba Linda, CA

Wife: Thelma (Patricia) Catherine Ryan

Children: Patricia, Julie

Vice President: 1st term and part of 2nd term Spiro T. Agnew; 2nd term Gerald R. Ford

Political Party: Republican

Died: April 22, 1994, in New York, NY

Like many presidents, **Richard M. Nixon** grew up in poverty. He worked hard in school and was offered scholarships to Harvard and Yale, but he felt he had to stay close to home for college. He got involved in student government and went on to law school.

When he was running for the Senate in 1950, Nixon earned the nickname Tricky Dick because of the tricks he used to win the election. Still, he was a successful politician and Eisenhower's vice president. In 1960, Nixon lost the election to JFK. He ran again in 1968 and won.

The nation was divided by the war in Vietnam and the struggle for civil rights when Nixon took office.

As president, Nixon improved the United States' relationships with China and the Soviet Union. He brought the troops home from Vietnam, and was in office when U.S. astronauts landed on the moon. But Nixon used tricks to make sure he was reelected in 1972. His men broke into Democratic Party offices to find secret information about Nixon's competition. Nixon lied about what he knew of the break-in. He resigned from office so that he wouldn't have to face a trial in the Senate.

When he became the only president in history to resign, the country was conflicted and people no longer trusted the government.

★ Agent Nixon?

Before he got involved in politics, Nixon wanted to be an FBI agent. The FBI didn't accept his application.

★ Strike!

Nixon liked bowling so much that he had a bowling alley installed in the White House.

★ Ping-Pong Diplomacy

The United States had cut all ties to China when the Communists took over the Chinese government in 1949. When the Chinese invited an American Ping-Pong team to compete in 1971, Nixon saw a chance to begin talking again. After many secret meetings between government officials, the president announced that he would visit China himself in 1972.

Gerald R. Ford

fact file

Born: July 14, 1913, in Omaha, NE

Wife: Elizabeth (Betty) Bloomer Warren

Children: Michael Gerald, John Gardner, Steven Meigs, Susan Elizabeth

Vice President: Nelson A. Rockefeller

Political Party: Republican

Died: December 26, 2006, in Rancho Mirage, CA

38th President
1974–1977

When **Gerald R. Ford** took office, many people had lost faith in government. Ford worked to restore their trust.

Ford never expected to be president. Born in Nebraska and raised in Michigan, he was a good student and a standout football player. He played college ball and went to Yale Law School, before joining the navy during World War II. Back home in Michigan, he was elected to Congress in 1948. He was still there twenty-five years later when Richard Nixon asked him to become vice president.

One of the first things Ford did as president was grant a full pardon to Nixon. That meant he excused Nixon for the crimes he committed. Many people were angry. They wanted Nixon to stand trial. Ford believed it was best for the country to move on.

The United States had other problems to deal with. The Cold War with the Soviet Union continued, and the economy was in bad shape. Prices were going up and jobs were hard to find. Ford's efforts to turn things around failed, and he battled with Congress at nearly every step.

In 1976, Ford ran for a second term, but lost to Jimmy Carter. He remains the only president in history who was not elected president or vice president by the American people.

★ Did You Know?

Ford's name was Leslie Lynch King Jr. when he was born. He was given his stepfather's name when he was two years old and later adopted by him. Ford wasn't told about the adoption until he was thirteen.

★ Strike a Pose!

Ford helped pay for law school by working as a fashion model. He was on the cover of *Cosmopolitan* magazine and in the pages of *Look*.

★ Touchdown!

Ford was an all-star football player at the University of Michigan. The Detroit Lions and the Green Bay Packers both wanted him to play professional football when he graduated, but Ford went to Yale Law School instead.

Jimmy Carter

39th President
1977–1981

fact file

Born: October 1, 1924, in Plains, GA

Wife: Eleanor Rosalynn Smith

Children: John William (Jack), James Earl III (Chip), Donnel Jeffrey (Jeff), Amy Lynn

Vice President: Walter Mondale

Political Party: Democrat

Died: Still alive

James Carter Jr. was always known as Jimmy, and that's how he was sworn in as president. Carter was a Washington outsider—someone who had never been involved in Washington politics. He promised never to lie to the American people.

Carter grew up on a peanut farm in Georgia, and sold boiled peanuts from a red wagon by the side of the road. After high school, Carter went to the Naval Academy and became a nuclear submarine engineer. When his father died, he took over the family farm, and later became governor of Georgia.

Almost no one outside of Georgia had heard of Carter when he decided to run for president. He campaigned for two years and won the 1976 election.

Carter's outsider standing made it difficult for him to work with Congress. There was an energy crisis with shortages of gasoline and high prices. Then, in 1979, sixty-six American diplomats were captured at the U.S. embassy in

Iran. All of Carter's efforts to free them failed. They weren't released until the day he left office.

Carter lost the 1980 election to Ronald Reagan, but he didn't retire quietly. He's written nearly thirty books. He also created the Carter Center, which works to improve human rights around the world and helps countries settle their differences peacefully. In 2002, he won the Nobel Peace Prize.

★ Presidential Firsts

Carter was the first American president to be born in a hospital. The others were born at home.

★ Did You Know?

When he was a boy, Carter shot his sister Gloria in the rear end with a BB gun after she threw a wrench at him. Of course, he was later was punished by his father!

★ House Hunter

Houses sold at rock-bottom prices during the Great Depression when Carter was a boy. Carter saved the money he earned and by the time he was thirteen, he bought five houses around Plains and rented them to families in the area.

Ronald W. Reagan

40th President
1981–1989

fact file

Born: February 6, 1911, in Tampico, IL

First Wife: Jane Wyman (divorced 1949); **Second Wife:** Nancy Davis (married 1952)

Children: Maureen Elizabeth, Michael Edward, Patricia Ann, Ronald Prescott

Vice President: George H. W. Bush

Political Party: Republican

Died: June 5, 2004, in Los Angeles, CA

Ronald W. Reagan grew up in small towns in Illinois. His family was poor and moved a lot, but young Reagan loved sports and acting. At college, he was on the football team and acted in plays. Afterward, he got a job as a radio announcer and became the most popular sports announcer in Iowa. Then he went to California and started an acting career. Reagan made fifty-two films and hosted a popular television program.

Along the way, he got interested in politics. In 1966, he was elected governor of California and served two terms. He wanted to run for president in 1968 and 1976, but both times the Republican Party chose other candidates. In 1980, he won the nomination, and the election.

When he took office, Reagan said he wanted to be the president "who made Americans believe in themselves again." He tried to improve the economy by cutting taxes and creating jobs. At the same time, he increased spending on the military to keep the United States safe. The government spent more money than it earned in taxes.

In his second term, Reagan worked to bring the Cold War to a peaceful end. When he left office in 1989, many people believed the world was a safer place.

★ College Bound

Reagan was the first member of his family to go to college. He worked his way through Eureka College working as a dishwasher and at other odd jobs.

★ Jelly Beans

Reagan loved jelly beans and kept a jar of them on his desk. When he became president, the Jelly Belly company started making a new flavor—blueberry—so that he would have red, white, and blue jelly beans at his inauguration parties. There is a picture of Reagan made from ten thousand jelly beans at the Ronald Reagan Presidential Library.

★ Reaganomics

Reagan believed in cutting taxes for the wealthy. He thought their savings would "trickle down" to the rest of the American people.

George H. W. Bush

41st President
1989–1993

fact file

Born: June 12, 1924, in Milton, MA

Wife: Barbara Pierce

Children: George Walker, Robin, John Ellis (Jeb), Neil, Marvin, Dorothy

Vice President: J. Danforth (Dan) Quayle III

Political Party: Republican

Died: Still alive

George H. W. Bush belonged to a political family. His father was a senator from Connecticut. Young Bush's wealthy parents taught him to serve his country. At boarding school, he was senior class president and captain of the baseball and soccer teams. On the day he graduated, he joined the navy to fight in World War II.

After the war, Bush went to Yale University and then moved to Texas to work in the oil industry. Like his father, he entered politics. He was a member of Congress, a representative to the United Nations and to China, and head of the CIA. Then he became Ronald Reagan's vice president. After two terms, he ran for president himself.

The world was changing when Bush became president. The Cold War ended and the Soviet Union split into a number of smaller countries. There were other trouble spots around the world. In 1989, Bush sent troops to Kuwait, an oil-rich country, to protect it from Iraq. Operation Desert Storm was a big victory for the U.S. and the United Nations.

At home, Bush was not as successful. The economy started to fail, and even though he had promised not to raise taxes, he did. In 1992, the American people voted for change.

★ Fearless Flyer

Bush was the navy's youngest pilot during World War II. He flew fifty-eight missions. On one mission, he was shot down over the Pacific and rescued by a submarine!

★ Presidential Pets

The Bush family's dog Millie became an author while the family was at the White House. *Millie's Book: As Dictated to Barbara Bush* was a bestseller.

★ Family Affair

George H. W. and George W. Bush are the second father-son pairs to be elected president. John and John Quincy Adams were the first.

William J. Clinton

42nd President
1993–2001

fact file

Born: August 19, 1946, in Hope, AR

Wife: Hillary Rodham

Children: Chelsea Victoria

Vice President: Albert Gore Jr.

Political Party: Democrat

Died: Still alive

President Clinton was born **William J. Blythe III**, three months after his father died in a car accident. His mother later married Roger Clinton, and Bill took his stepfather's name. His mother often told her son he would be president one day, and he believed her. As a teenager, Clinton had two main interests: politics and playing the saxophone.

Clinton went to Georgetown University and got involved in student government. Later he studied law at Yale, where he met his wife, Hillary Rodham. Clinton went back to Arkansas and entered politics. In 1978 he was the country's youngest governor, and in 1992 he ran for president and won.

Clinton focused on making the economy better and ensuring the government didn't spend more money than it took in. His plan was successful. For the first time in thirty years, the federal government had extra money. Overseas, Clinton worked to create peace in the Middle East and in Eastern Europe. He also increased U.S. trade with China.

Even though he was charged with illegal behavior, Clinton was popular when he left office. Today, the William J. Clinton Foundation helps people around the world. In addition, Clinton works with other former presidents to raise money for victims of disasters such as the earthquake in Haiti.

★ Did You Know?

During high school, Clinton went to a youth conference in Washington, DC, and shook JFK's hand in the Rose Garden.

★ Impeachment

Clinton was the second president in history to be impeached, or accused of breaking the law, by the House of Representatives. He lied about a relationship he had with a White House intern. Like Andrew Johnson, he was tried in the Senate and found not guilty.

★ First Lady

Hillary Rodham Clinton is the only First Lady to later be elected to the Senate. She wanted to run for president in 2008, but the Democratic Party nominated Barack Obama instead. She was later named secretary of state.

★ Presidential Firsts

Bill Clinton was the first president to be born after World War II.

George W. Bush

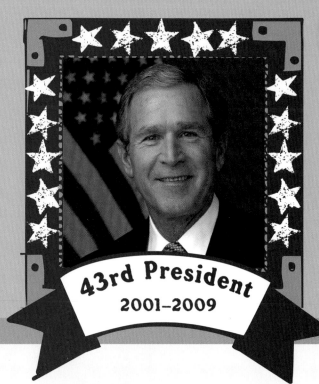

43rd President
2001–2009

fact file

Born: July 6, 1946, in New Haven, CT

Wife: Laura Welch

Children: Jenna, Barbara

Vice President: Richard (Dick) Cheney

Political Party: Republican

Died: Still alive

George W. Bush was not named the winner of the 2000 election, held on November 7, until December 12. The election was so close that votes in Florida and other states had to be recounted. Finally, the Supreme Court named George W. Bush the winner over former vice president Al Gore.

Bush grew up in a political family. His father was the forty-first president. Like his father, young Bush played baseball. After graduating from Yale and Harvard, he worked in the oil business and became governor of Texas.

President Bush cut taxes and won money for education programs in his first few months in office. Then the country was attacked on September 11, 2001. U.S. troops invaded Afghanistan to capture the terrorists. The Afghan government was overthrown.

Bush believed that the Iraqi government had weapons that threatened the United States. In 2003, the United States went to war, but the weapons were never found.

When he left office, American soldiers were still fighting in Afghanistan and Iraq. At home, banks were failing, gas prices had gone way up, and people were losing jobs. Bush retired to a ranch in Texas, where he wrote his bestselling memoir, *Decision Points*, about his years as president.

★ Play Ball!

Bush didn't get to fulfill his dream of becoming a major league baseball player, but he did become part owner of the Texas Rangers baseball team.

★ Barney Cam

One of President Bush's three dogs, Barney, wore a tiny camera on his collar for the holiday season in 2002. The video was put on the Internet, giving the world a dog's-eye view of the White House Christmas decorations.

★ Nicknames

After he was elected, Bush's father started calling him Quincy, after John Quincy Adams, as a joke. Other people called him W, pronounced "Dubya," to avoid confusion with his father.

Barack H. Obama

44th President
2009–

fact file

Born: August 4, 1961, in Honolulu, HI

Wife: Michelle Robinson

Children: Malia, Natasha (Sasha)

Vice President: Joseph Biden

Political Party: Democrat

Died: Still alive

Barack H. Obama made history when he was elected the first African American President of the United States. Obama's mother was a white woman from Kansas, and his father was a black man from Kenya. His parents met in college in Hawaii, where Obama was born.

His father left the family when young Obama was two. The future president lived in Indonesia for a few years with his mother and stepfather. His mother wanted him to get the best education, so he went back to Hawaii and lived with his grandparents. He was a good student and loved to play basketball.

Obama graduated from Columbia University and then worked in Chicago's poorest neighborhoods. He went on to receive a law degree from Harvard. Then he went back to Chicago to work with community organizations. He served in the Illinois State Senate and won election to the U.S. Senate in 2004.

Obama took office during a financial crisis, known as a recession, which was second only to the Great Depression. The United States was also fighting two wars in Afghanistan and Iraq. He has worked to fix the economy, improve the United States' reputation around the world, bring the troops home from Iraq, and pass a healthcare reform bill. It's too soon to know if his presidency will be called successful, or whether he will be elected for a second term.

★ White House Luau

President Obama made a small change to the annual White House picnic for the members of Congress and their families. He threw a luau, complete with flower leis, Hawaiian food, and hula dancers!

★ Nobel Peace Prize

Obama is the third president to win the Nobel Peace Prize while in office. Theodore Roosevelt was the first in 1906, followed by Woodrow Wilson in 1919. Jimmy Carter was awarded the prize after he left the White House.

★ Presidential Pets

On election night, Obama promised his daughters, Malia and Sasha, that they could have a puppy when they moved to the White House. The family chose a Portuguese water dog and named him Bo.

THE THREE BRANCHES OF GOVERNMENT

The men who met at the Constitutional Convention in 1787 wanted to create a strong central government. At the same time, they didn't want one person or group to have too much power. They divided the government into three equal branches. Each branch has its own job to do.

The **legislative** branch makes laws, decides how the government will spend its money, and must vote before the United States goes to war. This branch is made up of the Senate and the House of Representatives. Each state has two senators, who serve six-year terms of office. The number of representatives from each state is based on the size of its population. Representatives serve for two years. The people of their states elect members of Congress.

The president is in charge of the **executive** branch. The vice president and the president's close advisors, called his cabinet, are also part of the executive branch. The president signs bills, which then become laws. He or she may also veto, or reject, bills. The president chooses Supreme Court justices (who must be approved by the Senate) and is the commander in chief of the military. The president serves a four-year term, and can only serve for two terms, or a total of eight years.

The Supreme Court, the most powerful court in the country, is the head of the **judicial** branch of the government. The federal court decides arguments about the meanings of laws and decides whether those laws agree with the Constitution. Once they are appointed, the nine members, or justices, of the Supreme Court can stay on the Court for the rest of their lives.

The three branches of government work together to make sure the country runs smoothly.

HOW PRESIDENTS ARE ELECTED

In most non-presidential elections in the United States, voters cast their ballots for the candidate whom they want to win, and then the votes are counted. The winner is the person with the most votes.

Presidential elections are a two-step process. When Americans cast their votes for president, they are really voting for an elector. Together, these electors are known as the electoral college. Each state has as many electors as it has members of Congress. Another three electors represent the District of Columbia. Today there are 538 electors.

The candidate with the most popular votes wins all of that state's electoral votes. In order to become president, a candidate must win a majority (at least one more than half) of all the electoral votes, or at least 270.

The Founding Fathers set up the electoral college as a way to give states with small populations more of an equal weight in the election process.

In most presidential elections, the candidate with the popular vote also wins the electoral vote—but not always. George W. Bush lost the popular election by more than five hundred thousand votes, but won the electoral vote in 2000. Other presidents who were elected without winning the popular vote were John Quincy Adams, Rutherford B. Hayes, and Benjamin Harrison.

GLOSSARY

Abolitionist: A person who wants to put an end to slavery.

Ambassador: An official sent by one country to represent it in another country.

Bill of Rights: The first ten amendments to the U.S. Constitution. The Bill of Rights guarantees basic human rights, such as freedom of speech and freedom of religion.

Cabinet: The fifteen heads of departments of the government that are part of the executive branch. These include the departments of defense, education, and homeland security.

Confederate: A supporter of the Confederate States of America—the states that tried to leave the United States at the beginning of the Civil War.

Congress: The legislative body of the U.S. government—the group that makes laws. The U.S. Congress is made up of the Senate and the House of Representatives.

Congressperson: A member of Congress.

Constitution: The document that outlines how the U.S. government works. The highest law of the land.

Declaration of Independence: The statement adopted by the Continental Congress on July 4, 1776, which announced that the thirteen American colonies were independent and no longer a part of the British Empire.

Deficit: When the government spends more money than it earns in taxes, the difference is the deficit.

Democratic Party: The political party that grew out of the Democratic-Republican Party and is still active today. Andrew Jackson was the first Democratic president.

Democratic-Republican Party: A political party founded in the early 1790s by Thomas Jefferson and James Madison.

Diplomat: A person who represents a government in another country.

Election: The formal process of choosing (electing) who will hold a certain office, such as president or senator.

Electoral college: A group of electors chosen by the voters in each state to elect the president and vice president of the United States.

Electoral vote: The vote cast by the electoral college in a presidential election.

Executive: The branch of government that is led by the president, who signs bills into law and is commander in chief of the armed forces.

Federalist Party: A political party active from 1789 to 1801. Its supporters included George Washington and John Adams.

Founding Fathers: The political leaders of the United States who signed the Declaration of Independence and helped write the Constitution.

Free state: A state in which slavery is illegal.

Frontier: The farthest edge of settled land before wilderness begins. The American West is often referred to as the frontier.

Governor: The head of a state, elected by the people.

House of Representatives: The larger house of the U.S. Congress.

Impeach: To charge an elected official with illegal behavior. The House of Representatives has the power to impeach a president, which leads to a trial in the Senate.

Judicial: The branch of government that is primarily responsible for interpreting the law.

Legislative: The branch of government that is primarily responsible for writing and passing laws. The U.S. Congress.

Legislator: A person who makes laws.

Peace Corps: A volunteer program run by the government. The Peace Corps helps people and communities all over the world.

Political party: A group of people who share certain political beliefs. Political parties try to influence the government by getting members of their party elected.

Popular vote: The votes cast for a candidate made by all of the voters.

Population: All of the people living in a particular city, state, or country.

President: The leader of the government's executive branch.

Representative: A member of the House of Representatives.

Republican Party: A political party founded by abolitionists in 1854. It came into power in 1860 with the election of Abraham Lincoln and is still active today.

Senate: The smaller house of the U.S. Congress. The Senate has some powers that the House of Representatives does not, such as agreeing to treaties proposed by the president.

Senator: A member of the Senate.

Slave state: A state in which owning slaves is legal.

Tax: Money charged by a government to run a city, state, or federal government. Taxes are often a percentage of a person's income or property, such as real estate.

Term of office: The length of time a person serves in a particular office before a new election is held. The president's term is four years.

Territory: An area of land under the control of a government.

Union: An organization of states with the same central government. The United States is often referred to as the Union.

United Nations: An international organization that works to bring about cooperation between countries, human rights, and world peace.

Veto: To reject a law or a proposal made by the U.S. Congress.

Vice president: The government official chosen by and elected along with the president, who takes over the presidency if the president dies or leaves office.

Whig Party: A political party active from the 1830s to the 1850s. Millard Fillmore was the last Whig to hold the office of president.

SOURCES

BOOKS

Bausum, Ann. *Our Country's Presidents: All You Need to Know about the Presidents, from George Washington to Barack Obama*. Washington, DC: National Geographic, 2009.

Beschloss, Michael R., ed. *The American Heritage Illustrated History of the Presidents*. New York: Crown, 2000.

Beyer, Rick. *The Greatest Presidential Stories Never Told: 100 Tales from History to Astonish, Bewilder, and Stupefy*. New York: HarperCollins, 2007.

Additional resources were consulted for individual essays, including biographies and Internet sites.

WEBSITES

There are a number of reliable online resources for information about the presidents.

American President: An Online Reference Resource, Miller Center of Public Affairs at the University of Virginia
http://millercenter.org/president

The Library of Congress: Presidents of the United States: Research Guides
http://www.loc.gov/rr/program/bib/presidents/index.html

The National Park Service: American Presidents
http://www.nps.gov/history/nr/travel/presidents/

PBS's American Experience: The Presidents
http://www.pbs.org/wgbh/amex/presidents/01_washington/index.html

The White House: The Presidents
http://www.whitehouse.gov/about/presidents